CW00471285

The Book of
Many Colours

Awaken Your Soul's Purpose
with the Divine Rays

Angela Orora Medway-Smith

Cariad Spiritual

Dedication

This book is dedicated to my darling husband and soulmate, Ian, whose unwavering support and belief in me made it all possible.

Contents

"Are You Ready?"

"This is your time – the time of enlightenment.

You can choose whether to sit, remain in your current position and be blind to the possibilities or to embrace them.

As always, it is your choice.

The balance of existing in this human world or soaring with all the gifts of your spirit are your choices.

Choose wisely, dear ones; your future and indeed the future of all sentient beings depends on this choice.

Where do we begin with your instruction? The information you will find on these pages is not new. I and my brothers and sisters have delivered it through many channels, many times.

You will find it presented here in a simplified fashion – as needed at this time – in order for it to be accessible to mankind as a whole in this new age.

Your planet is fragile, and so is your species. So many gifts have been bestowed upon you that have gone unused, wasted or exploited.

It is not too late; indeed, it is NOW that is the time to become fully awake, to utilise these gifts for the benefit of ALL."

The Ascended Master St Germain

Channelled by Angela Orora, August 2020

Preface

This book is a practical handbook; a jumping-off point of discovery in what I hope will be for you the beginning of a relationship with some of the most highly evolved beings in our Universe.

They want YOU to connect with them. They want to support you, bring you knowledge, share their wisdom. You have been drawn to this book for a reason. Your Soul is seeking to grow.

Wherever you are on your journey of spiritual discovery, please don't skip the **Before You Begin** section. It contains important information for your safety, comfort and protection.

First, let me share with you how this book came about. I was told I was to write this book by a lovely angel channeller called Sarah Haywood in the summer of 2019; I was even given the title. This was news to me, as at that time, I had no idea what the book was to be about and even less idea that I was not the author, simply the channel. I had never had any intention of writing a book.

So, let me tell you a little about me. I was born in a small Welsh fishing village in the early 1960s, raised in a family of strong women with four generations living under the same roof. Uncles, aunts and cousins filled the surrounding streets. Our door was always open. We were poor in financial terms, grew our own vegetables, kept chickens, ate the fish caught by my uncle, wore handmade clothes and hand-me-downs but were rich, so rich in love. If you've ever read Dylan Thomas' *Under Milk Wood,* that will give you an idea of Welsh village life in that era!

A strong faith was imbued in me. As a child, I went to church and Sunday school three times on a Sunday at Welsh Methodist and

Anglican churches. I was taught that God was everywhere, and my overriding 'training', I guess you would call it, is that Jesus wanted me for a sunbeam! I saw spirit as a child, and when I told my mother and grandmother, I was never chastised. They simply nodded and smiled, and I was made to feel that it was perfectly normal, although not to be talked about.

Being a psychic child was difficult. Many of you readers will probably understand this, always feeling that you don't quite fit in. While I joined with other children swimming down at the beach and harbour, in the park or on long walks, my evenings were spent buried in a book or another world with my spirit companions.

Fast forward to 1983; I was 19 and announced to my mother that I was moving to London with plans of travelling the world. My path, however, kept me there for almost a decade and brought me to a wonderful teacher of healing and spiritual development, Betty Balcombe.

I began to rediscover my psychic gifts and my connection with spirit. I took Betty's development course and then sat in circle with her every week at her home in Surrey for seven years. She gave me encouragement and permission to teach her course, which I did initially in Australia in 1990. Then in 1993, I was taken back to Wales to meet my wonderful husband Ian and raise our two children.

Looking back, every choice I have made, every job I have held has prepared me and brought me to where I am today. I have worn many hats, but the theme throughout my life has been to be that 'sunbeam'; working in the background, supporting people to be the best they can, by organising conferences, running a mental health charity, helping people to set up their own businesses and several other roles until finally, trusting that my ultimate role as a spiritual teacher and channel is the one that I set out on this life journey to accomplish.

I am here to enable, inspire and support people on their own journey of healing and spiritual discovery, and to transform their lives and soar to their Soul's highest potential.

I set up Cariad Spiritual back in 2016 to bring healing, guidance, and light to my little corner of Wales. Cariad is the Welsh word for love or sweetheart, and I chose this name for my business because it reflected how I approach my work. Passionate about making healing and holistic therapies accessible in my town, I raised money for charity by organising Spiritual and Holistic Festivals, Mind Body Spirit Fayres, and holding weekly healing events. I also ran intuitive development and healing training courses, workshops, and classes to support people along their own spiritual development path. For a time, I also worked in London as a spiritual consultant at the world-famous esoteric bookshop 'Mysteries of Covent Garden'. Regularly travelling 200 miles between West Wales and London was exhausting but rewarding (my teenage son had moved to London, and I wasn't ready to let him go completely!).

Spirit, the Angels, the Universe, God or whomever you want to call the forces that guide us have other plans for me, which brings me back to this book. I was guided by St Germain to gather a small group to support the channelling of this work.

The Ascended Masters St Germain and Lord Lanto, in particular, are very keen that this information reaches more people, that more beautiful souls are empowered and enlightened by accessing the Divine Rays using simple, practical techniques.

The Divine Rays have been accessible to mankind since the time of Lemuria; in our recent history, this information has been kept hidden, and even when the great channels Madame Blavatsky, Guy Ballard and Alice Bailey made this information available, it was still inaccessible to most.

So, here it is, a practical handbook to help you access and enjoy communion with the Divine Rays and their patrons; a source of healing, knowledge, and increased wisdom, a journey, I hope, that will bring you much joy and wisdom.

I feel truly blessed that the Ascended Masters have chosen me, amongst many other lightworkers, as their mouthpiece. I hope you enjoy their words, find comfort, strength and inspiration on these pages and are able to translate your intention into action for the benefit of ALL.

Brightest and abundant blessings,

Angela Orora Medway-Smith

"Heaven is not a place to go to, dear ones. It is a state of consciousness that you can embrace and create for yourself at any time, even in your dimension. When you develop it, you can easily create for yourself, no matter what is taking place around you, a true state of heaven on earth in which you can experience life as gracious, abundant, calm and without limitation."

The Judge, The Seven Sacred Flames

Aurelia Louise Jones

Introduction

Scientists agree that everything, 'ALL that there is', you, the chair you sit on, our beloved planet is simply made of atoms and molecules that vibrate at different rates.

The light, sound, and energy vibrations - such as the different frequency waves which carry data that floods our planet - are equally made up of different vibrations.

This is not a scientific book nor an academic study. There will be no detailed explanation of frequency and its effect on 'All that there is'.

The information that is contained in this book is not new. It is very simply ancient teaching presented in an accessible way for the 21st century. The Patrons of the Divine Rays who channelled this book have worked with many other mediums and channels to remind us that we all have the ability to access these frequencies; however, much of this material is not readily usable or accessible.

Additionally, there have been shifts and changes in the quality of this vibrational energy and the availability of rays and energies not previously accessible to humankind.

This and the preceding century have seen great advances in vibrational medicine. There have been countless academic studies, and there is broad acceptance by scientists and the medical profession alike of the benefit to ourselves and 'ALL that there is', of both ancient and modern vibrational medicine, from colour, sound, crystal and pure energy vibration channelled by other human beings. Indeed, it was Albert Einstein that said:

"Future medicine will be the medicine of frequencies."

With these facts at hand, please open your mind to the power of the Divine Rays, the primary vibrational essences of our Universe, each of which holds a unique frequency.

A special mention goes to the wonderful Edwin Courtenay, who has been working with the Ascended Masters and Angelic Realm for many years. St Germain himself, who patronises us both, advised me not to 'reinvent the wheel', that information on the current status of the Divine Rays had already been gifted to mankind channelled by Edwin from St Germain.

The pages that follow contain my channellings from the Ascended Masters, Archangels, and Angelic Collectives that serve on the Divine Rays. Some will be very familiar old friends, others new acquaintances; all of them serve the Creator of All that there is and step forward from these pages to support you.

There are lots of different ways that you can choose to connect with these energies. You may choose meditation, prayer or invocation, visualisation, or perhaps connect with images of the beings that patronise the Divine Rays. I have included some ideas on how to connect, but I would encourage you to follow your own intuition in this, as in all things.

You may wish to digest this book in a few hours, then return to a point as guided by your intuition, to dip in and out, or to work systematically with each Divine Ray following a 28 Ray immersion or any other way that feels right to you.

Whatever you do, my view is that working with these energies and the presences that govern them can bring you huge benefits. The only limitation is your intention.

I see communion with the Divine Rays as nectar for the mind, body, and soul; remember what Albert Einstein said!

Part One

Before You Begin

"A journey of a thousand miles begins with a single step."

Lao Tzu

Spiritual Protection

Would you leave your front door wide open while you are asleep? Would you walk out in a storm without a coat?

Similarly, it is just not sensible to begin any spiritual practice without considering protection. Spiritual or psychic protection is an essential first step before opening the door to the spirit world or beginning any spiritual practice.

It was the first thing I was taught as a complete novice, and it is the first thing I teach my students, quite simply to prevent attracting any negative energy.

Spiritual protection is not complicated; it simply involves requesting protection from higher powers before you begin any spiritual work. In fact, I don't start my day or get out of bed without calling in my guides and Guardian Angel.

There are hundreds and hundreds of prayers, rituals, or invocations you can choose from, or you could use visualisation instead. In my experience, a personal prayer can be very powerful, so I would encourage you to write your own. However, here is a simple prayer or invocation you can use if you prefer:

Simple Daily Protection

Divine Spirit, Creator of All,

I call forth now my guides and Ministering Angels,

To draw close, to bring me guidance and protection,

Now, and until I leave this Earthly realm

Amen (or any ending you prefer)

Here is a simple visualisation that you can use to protect your space and yourself before you start a spiritual practice:

Divine Protection Visualisation

Visualise a pinpoint of divine energy from the Creator in the centre of the room in front of you.

Begin to expand this point of energy until it grows to the size of a golf ball, an orange, a football, a beach ball, and increase the size of this sphere of divine light until it completely encircles you.

It then fills the room you are in, reaching into every corner.

It fills your home and expands further until it reaches out into every corner of your garden, into the street.

On the outside of this sphere of divine light, place the colour platinum to repel negativity.

This platinum layer can be as light as gossamer silk or as heavy as a coat of platinum paint on days you feel a bit more vulnerable.

On days where you may feel vulnerable (we all have these), you can layer up your spiritual protection with prayer, visualisation and also by carrying crystals that have a protective energy.

On the whole, the Law of Attraction ensures that we attract what we put out into the Universe.

If you think negative thoughts, you attract negative energy and experiences, so it follows that if you think positive thoughts, you attract the positive. (If you do want to delve deeper into psychic protection, there is a fabulous book by Caitlin Matthews.)

Managing your Energy

We are all unique beings. We all vibrate at different rates. We all have a different capacity for channelling spiritual energy, and it is really important that you are aware of the effect of these different vibrations on your physical and energetic body. Learn to listen to your body and how it responds to different frequencies.

Special care is needed by those of you with diabetes. You will notice that channelling spiritual energy draws on your reserves, so please be careful. Even with almost forty years of experience channelling different spiritual energies, I sometimes still get caught out!

Journaling

Keeping a journal is a really helpful practice. That way, you can track your progress and express your gratitude for the energies as you begin to work with the Divine Rays, checking in with yourself on a regular basis, seeing how you are developing, how your life is changing. You can decide on what you want to record and how you measure the changes.

For a free downloadable spiritual journal to record your experiences with the Divine Rays, go to my website https://www.cariadspiritual.com/divinerays.

Energetic Tools & Techniques

I'd like to talk here about visualisation, crystals, colours, symbols, shapes and sacred geometry. These are all enormous subjects, and you will find thousands of books, huge encyclopaedias, and literally tons of information on the internet on each and every one of them.

I'm mentioning them here because you can use each of these tools to connect better with the Divine Rays.

All of these subjects can be studied individually, and the techniques and information that you learn will most definitely benefit you in your spiritual development.

I would encourage you to follow your intuition, be discerning, find authors whose energy you align with, find tools and methods that suit you and absorb what you need.

If I had to choose one book to recommend on visualisation, it would be *Creative Visualisation* by Shakti Gawain. This little book changed my life. I came across it in about 1983 and have probably possessed a dozen copies since; I think it is so wonderful I keep giving my copy away to friends!

I have added a bit about crystals in Part Four; however, my go-to crystal experts are Judy Hall and Philip Permutt, who have both published dozens of helpful books. I would also highly recommend Edwin Courtenay's *Crystals to Go*.

Prayer, Invocation, Ritual and Affirmation

I love this quote from St Teresa of Avila, a 16th century Spanish mystic talking about prayer as:

"...an intimate friendship,

a frequent conversation held alone with the Beloved."

Prayer, invocation, ritual, and affirmation are individually incredible spiritual tools used by humans throughout the ages.

Put very simply, prayer is an invocation or act that seeks to activate a rapport with an object of worship through deliberate communication.

When we pray, repeat an invocation, repeat an affirmation, or perform a ritual of any kind, we are communicating, making a request, or perhaps setting an intention.

Physical changes occur within our brain and our physiology, and on a quantum level, we send a pulse of vibratory energy towards the 'object'. We are back to vibration again!

It then follows that because of The Law of Attraction, what we receive back from this 'pulse of energy' depends on our own vibration.

This is my personal understanding, a very simplistic view of a hugely complex subject. But what I am trying to explain here is that we will all have a different experience connecting with the Divine Rays.

I also believe that no experience is less than the other, that we receive what we need at the time and that this experience will change over time as we change and develop. So, consider creating your own prayer, invocation or ritual using the words that feel right to you.

The patrons have given us affirmations for each of the Divine Rays, but if you are guided to tweak them, do. This is YOUR practice, be guided by your intuition and discernment.

Past Life Recall

When you connect with the Divine Rays, many of you will experience past life recall and remembrance. I would encourage you to journal these recollections and not worry too much about them to start with, as the Patrons have a way of helping you to understand through serendipity and portent.

Reincarnation and Past Lives are other subjects that hundreds of books have been written about. My first 'teacher' on this subject was Edgar Cayce, and his books are a good place to start if you want a better understanding of the subject.

If you do feel a need to make more sense of these experiences, the best guidance you will find is from your own Spirit Guides and Guardian Angel; simply connect with them in prayer or meditation and ask what you need to know.

Gratitude & Aftercare

It is only polite to say please and thank you! Do remember to ask to connect and thank your guides and guardians for their support and the Patrons of the Rays for connecting with you. Their service to us is a divine privilege.

You also need to take care moving from spiritual work back into the everyday world. After every spiritual practice, it is important to ground, centre and reset your energy system to a safe operating level. I tell my students to think of it like hitting the standby button on their TV.

Take some deep breaths, breathe down into the earth, centre yourself, move your body, take a drink of water or eat something, and call in your usual spiritual protection and your Guardian Angel.

Part Two

What It's All About

"I live, move, and have my Being and all outer expression in the full opulence of God, made manifest every moment."

St. Germain, The "I AM" Discourses
Guy Ballard 1935

What Are the Divine Rays?

In simple terms, the highest vibrating form of light is pure, clear light and that is the light of the Creator, the 'Divine'. Each Ray represents a different quality of the Divine, their energy present here on Earth.

At this point, it is important to note that the Rays have changed with time, as our planet has changed and as we have changed. Madame Blavatsky, Guy Ballard, Alice Bailey, Aurelia Louise Jones, and other great channels have written about the Rays and their functions, and if you feel guided to, research their work further and exercise your own discernment. Intuitively make up your own mind and select your own truth as to the current status of the Rays.

So, every schoolchild knows that when you shine a light through a clear crystal, a rainbow of coloured light is refracted through it, and we are all familiar with the colours of the rainbows that light our skies after the rain.

Similarly, the colours of the Divine Rays are the aspects of the Divine, energy that radiates down to our planet for the purpose of supporting All that there is. What follows in these pages is practical guidance on how to tap into this energy, together with a personal message from the Patrons of the Rays.

Each Divine Ray has a unique number, name, properties, colour, symbol, patron, active principle, and a crystal energy that aligns with it. (There are also Archangels, Archaea and other light beings that serve on the Rays, but I intend to keep it simple.)

This book covers 28 Divine Rays, from the Divine Ray system given in the Masters' channellings to Edwin Courtenay, that are of particular benefit to mankind at this time.

(I asked St Germain why I am only to bring you 28 and was told that more information will be given when we are ready for it!)

Who Are The Patrons of The Divine Rays?

There is a spiritual hierarchy that governs and supports life in our Universe and on this planet, which functions as a complex government. This is yet another huge subject, but very simply, the light beings that fulfil the roles of Patrons of the Divine Rays are Cosmic Ascended Masters, Ascended Masters, Lady Ascended Masters and Archangels. The beings who occupy these important roles as Patrons of the Divine Rays are considered to be among the most highly evolved beings in our Universe.

Don't let fear of being worthy put you off here. If you've picked up this book then you are ready to work with these energies and magnificent beings of light. No matter where you are on your spiritual journey connecting to these energies will bring wisdom and light into your life. Believe me, your life will never be the same again!

I won't be going into long descriptions about each of the Patrons. There is so much information readily available, but what I would say is, be discerning about what you accept as truth. Much of the information you will find in books and online is simply out of date, incorrect, plagiarised and adapted for gain.

How To Choose Which Ray To Connect With

There are several ways you can choose which Ray to work with. This list is not exhaustive, it simply represents ideas on ways that you can choose to work with the Rays' energy, and you should always be guided intuitively on what feels right for you (or your client if you are already an established energy healer or channel):

- ❀ Intuitively, by asking for guidance and simply by opening this book
- ❀ By choosing a Patron you feel particularly drawn to
- ❀ By choosing a colour you are drawn to
- ❀ By first choosing (or being chosen by) a crystal – you will find a quick list in Part Four - and connect to the Ray that aligns with this crystalline energy
- ❀ By choosing a symbol that 'jumps out at you'
- ❀ By identifying an issue you would like support with
- ❀ Intuitively selecting a particular Divine Ray to channel healing energy to another person, animal, or place
- ❀ Meditating on the message from the Patron
- ❀ For a really deep connection, by following a 28 Ray immersion practice.

Oracle cards will be available shortly from www.cariadspiritual.com to accompany this book and can be of further assistance in selecting which Divine Ray to work with Alternatively, you can use a numerological system called Ascension Numerology to determine your (or your client's) Destiny Ray.

Ascension Numerology & Your Destiny Ray

There are several different types of Numerology Systems which have been influenced by the culture of the society they originated in, such as Chaldean Numerology, Kabbalah Numerology, Tamil Numerology and Western Pythagorean Numerology.

Each type of Numerology has its own way of interpreting numbers and drawing out inferences. Very distinct, special and unique information is expressed in each type of Numerological System, which in turn helps people to know more about themselves.

Ascension Numerology is a system that was channelled from the Ascended Master St Germain through Edwin Courtenay over a period of 25 years, and working with it offers insight and guidance specific to the individual. One of its aspects is the Destiny Ray Number.

The Destiny Ray Number

The Destiny Ray Number represents your 'ray of incarnation' – the manifestation of Divine Energy that your Soul has chosen to incarnate under in this lifetime.

This is the energy, the Divine Ray, which your incarnating Spirit 'rides down' on and which governs and guides your life path and purpose.

Your Destiny Ray also grants you access to certain powers and energies so that you may fulfil your purpose within this life on Earth, as well as helping you through the support of and alignment to the Ray's governing Ascended Master or Archangel.

Although the Destiny Ray does not represent the entirety of your life path and purpose, it does, however, represent a significant aspect and element of it. It can be transcended by those who complete their obligations in this incarnation, but it will still influence the nature of your experiences and your spiritual development.

It is calculated as follows:

- Write down your date of birth – for example, John was born on the 19th of October 1962
- Now convert it into just number – 19/10/1962
- Now add all these separate numerals together – 1+9+1+0+1+9+6+2 = 29
- If the resulting number ends in a zero – 10, 20, 30, 40 … etc., or is a double number 11, 22, 33, 44, etc., KEEP IT!
- However, if it is anything else, reduce it further, so 29 becomes 2+9=11. Consequently, John's Destiny number is 11.

There are several things that are important regarding your Destiny Number:

- The colour of the Ray is something you can use. Wearing it or visualising it when you are feeling a little lost will help to pull you back upon your path.

- The shape or symbol can also be used in a similar way. If it is a shape, visualise it in three dimensions around you as a sacred space or if it is a symbol, visualise or wear a representation of that symbol. Equally, having it around you in your home or meditation room can help you better connect to both the Ray and, more importantly, its Patron.

- The properties are, of course, key in helping you to ascertain more regarding your destiny and purpose in this life.

❀ The Patron is possibly the most important aspect of the Ray, as this is likely to be your Master or Patron; the Ascended Master or Archangel who watches over you, guiding and supporting you by acting as your teacher on the road.

❀ Finally, the crystal can also help you to align with your path, purpose, and this energy and will assist you in drawing strength and power from your Destiny Ray.

It takes just a moment to calculate your Destiny Ray Number. However, the rewards can be infinite in terms of spiritual growth and alignment and flow on your life's path!

How To Connect With The Divine Rays

Getting Ready For Meditation

We all lead such busy lives in the 21st century, and for most of us, our minds are constantly busy. What we aim for in meditation is calming the 'monkey mind', learning to find quiet and space to allow divine connection. I do not want to preach to the converted, but if you have never meditated before, here are some helpful tips:

Find a comfortable space where you will not be disturbed. Turn off any unnecessary electronic gadgets and move them to another room. Get comfy and prepare to sit or lie still for a few minutes. If you are brand new to meditation, start with 10 minutes and work your way up. Eventually, aim for half an hour.

This is about the right amount of time for most people to connect to high vibrational energy.

Tip

Gather any appropriate crystals and place them nearby. You might like a pillow or blanket to hand, and remember to have a glass of water ready. It's also a good idea to set an alarm.

Bathing in sacred sound is a beautiful way to settle into your connection. I am a huge fan of the Solfeggio frequencies, the frequencies of our universe in sound, and there are so many free tracks available on YouTube. Be intuitive about your selection. Good ones to start with are 432 Hertz and 528 Hertz tracks.

Tip

Use headphones to block out any external noise and distractions. It's also helpful to have an electromagnetic shield if you're using a mobile phone. Shungite is a fantastic crystal for this; be mindful of the supplier of any crystal you purchase. Please ensure it has been ethically sourced.

Being cocooned in sacred oil vibrations during your connection is a glorious addition to this practice. Again, be intuitive in your selection and ensure that any oils you use are of the highest quality affordable.

Tip

I have a range of sacred meditation oil blends available on my website (www.cariadspiritual.com) to be used in oil burners or diffusers, the recipes for which have been channelled, which are attuned to the Divine Rays and their crystal counterparts.

Remember your Spiritual Protection (see page 10).

If you are unfamiliar with the human subtle body system, there are lots of images online which can help you visualise it.

Decide which Divine Ray you wish to connect to. Make a note of the crystal as this is the crystal that you will use to ground your energy during the meditation, and now set your intention.

Tip

It's always useful to set a specific intention. Actually having something measurable to aim for can be really useful.

Follow the channelled meditation script below.

Tip

Feel free to record this on your mobile phone or device while playing sacred music in the background if you wish. There are also pre-recorded meditations available on my website, www.cariadspiritual.com.

The Relaxation

We will use the breath to relax deeply and move relaxation through the physical body by way of the energy centres (chakras) preparing you for this connection.

Cleansing, clearing, relaxing, releasing, healing and harmonising, connecting you to 'All that there is, relaxing the physical, and shifting any negative or stuck energy in the subtle energy body.

Take at least two breaths at each chakra, be intuitive if you need to release more tension or stuck energy, then do so and feel the energy flow downwards.

It is useful to visualise the chakras as Catherine Wheels, seeing sparks of stuck energy drifting away to be grounded into Mother Earth, to be repurposed, recycled, and reused.

Divine Rays Connection Channelled Meditation

Make your body comfortable, roll back your shoulders and gently move your neck to release any tension. Make sure that your arms and legs are uncrossed, and if sitting, connect your feet with the floor beneath you.

Breathe deeply. In through your nose and out through your mouth, deep into your lungs. For a moment, simply be aware of the rise and fall of your belly.

Now, deepen the relaxation.

Breathe in for the count of three, hold for three, breathe out for three. (Repeat three times.)

Breathe in for the count of four, hold for four, breathe out for four. (Repeat three times.)

Start to feel waves of relaxation moving down over your physical body, starting at your Crown, the top of your head. Expand this chakra with your breath, cleansing, clearing, relaxing, releasing, healing, and harmonising. See the chakra spinning, clearing any stuck energy, and watch it rain down upon the Earth. Take as many breaths as you need before you move your breath with intention, down your body to the next chakra. Feel these waves begin to relax every hair on your head.

Move these waves of relaxation with your breath, down to your Brow Chakra in the centre of your forehead, your Third Eye. Expand this chakra with your breath, cleansing, clearing, relaxing, releasing, healing, and harmonising. See the chakra spinning, clearing any stuck energy, and watch it rain down upon the Earth. Take as many breaths as you need before you move your breath with intention down your body.

Move your attention to your Throat Chakra in the centre of your throat. Expand this chakra with your breath, cleansing, clearing, relaxing, releasing, healing, and harmonising. See the chakra spinning, clearing any stuck energy, and watch it rain down upon the Earth. Take as many breaths as you need before you move your breath with intention down your body.

Attend now to the shoulders, arms, hands, and fingers. Release any tension, allowing your breath to travel down, releasing tension, feeling it drifting away, returning it to Mother Earth.

Move your attention to your Heart Chakra in the centre of your chest. Expand this chakra with your breath, cleansing, clearing, relaxing, releasing, healing, and harmonising. See the chakra spinning, clearing any stuck energy, and watch it rain down upon the Earth. Take as many breaths as you need before you move your breath with intention down your body.

Move down to your Solar Plexus Chakra a few inches above your tummy button. Expand this chakra with your breath, cleansing, clearing, relaxing, releasing, healing, and harmonising. See the chakra spinning, clearing any stuck energy, and watch it rain down upon the Earth. Take as many breaths as you need before you move your breath with intention down your body.

Move down to your Sacral Chakra in the core of your belly. Expand the chakra with your breath, cleansing, clearing, relaxing, releasing, healing, and harmonising. See the chakra spinning, clearing any stuck energy, and watch it rain down upon the Earth. Take as many breaths as you need before you move your breath with intention down your body.

Move next to your Root Chakra at the base of your spine. Expand the chakra with your breath, cleansing, clearing, relaxing, releasing, healing, and harmonising. See the chakra spinning, clearing any stuck energy and watching it rain down upon the Earth. Take as many breaths as you need before you move your breath with intention down your body.

Now, draw this relaxing energy down your thighs, past your knees, shins, calves, ankles, feet, and toes, grounding all remaining negative or stuck energy into Mother Earth to be repurposed, recycled, reborn.

Take a moment now to ground yourself by imagining roots emanating from the soles of your feet and moving deeply into Mother Earth, weaving through the layers of earth, water, rock, and crystal until they reach the centre of the Earth and the crystal of the Divine Ray you have chosen to connect with.

Now, bring into your Mind's Eye the shape or symbol associated with the Divine Ray. If it is a shape, visualise that shape around you and transform it into three dimensions so that you are sitting within it. If it is a symbol, visualise that symbol in front of you and draw it in towards you, allowing it to rest where it feels comfortable.

Next, start to breathe the energy of the Divine Ray Crystal up through your roots through your Earth Star Chakra into your feet, feeling it travelling up your legs and into each of the lower chakras, your Root Chakra, with the next breath your Sacral Chakra, with the next breath your Solar Plexus Chakra, moving with the next breath up into your Heart Chakra where the energy rests.

Now send your intention upwards to the Creator and summon the Divine Ray of your choosing, breathing the energy down through your transpersonal chakras, the Stellar Gateway, and Soul Star Chakras above your head, into your Crown Chakra, filling it with Divine Ray Energy.

On the next breath, it moves with your breath filling your Brow Chakra, on the next breath to fill your Throat Chakra, until it finally comes to rest, filling and expanding in your Heart Chakra.

The energy of the Divine Ray, of the Creator and the divine crystalline energy you have drawn up from Mother Earth mix and merge, begin to swirl and expand in your Heart with your breath.

Now, with each breath you take, this Divine Energy expands. With your first breath, it expands out into your Throat and Solar Plexus Chakras. With your next breath, it expands into your Third Eye and Sacral Chakras, next your Crown and Root Chakras, next to your Soul Star and Earth Star Chakras above your head and beneath your feet.

This Divine Energy fills your physical and subtle energy body, now expanding out into your Auric Field, filling your Etheric Body, your Emotional Body, your Mental Body, your Astral Body, expanding further until it completely encompasses you in the Divine Ray Energy. Sitting within this earthly temple of the energy of the Divine Ray, it is time to request communion with the Patron of the Ray.

Repeat the Divine Ray Affirmation

With joy in your heart and gratitude for this sacred communion, call upon their presence and make your request.

For some of you, this experience will be clairvoyant, for others, clairaudient, and for some, the message may make itself known over the following days in serendipity, signs, or messages.

If you are recording this script for yourself, pause for a few moments while you allow yourself to experience this communion.

With deepest gratitude for this communion, give thanks to the Patron who has graced you with their presence. It is now time to return from your journey.

Begin to take some deeper breaths. Breathing deeply, start to be aware of your physical body and the chair that is supporting you. Wriggle your fingers, wriggle your toes, stretch and yawn.

Make sure you are properly grounded by breathing some energy into your Solar Plexus (if you are properly grounded, rewind those energetic roots that you sent into Mother Earth) and when you are ready, open your eyes.

Give thanks to all of the beings of light that have supported you on this journey, ground yourself, call in your usual spiritual protection and take a sip of water.

Note: You are responsible for managing your own energy, and it is important that you are fully present and grounded before going out into the world.

The 28 Ray Challenge

For complete immersion in the energy of the Divine Rays, you may wish to complete a 28 Ray Challenge, working with the energy of a different Ray each day, completely immersing yourself in this energy.

Don't feel obligated to do this challenge for 28 days straight. If you need to take a day off, a week off or repeat a day, just go with the flow and take this challenge at your own pace. It is about enjoying the journey rather than racing to the finishing post!

I cannot stress enough the importance of recording your experiences by journaling!

I have created a community on Facebook so you can share this journey with other seekers of Divine Ray energy. It can be found here:

https://www.facebook.com/groups/193813969564198

I always feel it's wonderful to be able to share experiences openly; I've created this group so that this can happen and so that we can all share with each other in a safe and open forum.

In Part Three, you will find detailed information about the Divine Rays, a channelled message from each of the Patrons, its colour, symbol or shape, properties, active principles (i.e. the flame - The Violet Flame of the 7th Divine Ray), its crystal counterpart and affirmation. There is so much information and inspiration from the Patrons on the following pages!

Remember, your spiritual journey is not a race. It is a lifelong road of twists and turns, of diversions, potholes, stop signs and speed bumps. YOU choose how to experience it. This ancient Irish blessing is my wish for you:

May the road rise up to meet you.
May the wind be always at your back.
May the sun shine warm upon your face;
the rains fall soft upon your fields
and until we meet again,
May God hold you in the palm of His hand.

Part Three

The Divine Rays

"Dearest children of my heart, 'blessed be' those of you whose heart has chosen an interest in becoming way-showers to the children of Earth. Blessed is the Light that glimmers through the folds of your individual soul, the motivating power which impels you forward, and which keeps your feet upon the pathway of Light."

The Cosmic Ascended Master Maitreya
The Seven Sacred Flames
Aurelia Louise Jones, 2007

The 1st Ray
The Ray of the Avatar

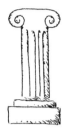

Patron: The Master Jesus

Colour: Ruby Red

Shape: The Single Pillar

Properties: Manifestation, energetic grounding, anchoring and embodiment. The Ray of the 'Master Builder'. Those who incarnate under this ray do so in order to create something meaningful and powerful for the world. Alignment and communion with the Divine Father, self-mastery through dedication, service, ritual, and practice. The masculine Christ energy the Christos – Passion. The Animus – masculine self.

Active Principle: The Flame of Divine Service (incorporating Divine Surrender and Divine Love)

Crystal: Ruby

Affirmation: I AM A SPARK OF THE DIVINE

The Master Jesus / Sananda speaks:

Children of the world, dear souls, I ask you not to worship me but what I stand for.

I implore you to love one another.

This simple action brings healing to all.

Love and forgive in love.

My message is very simple, let it be so.

The 2nd Ray
The Ray of Grace

Patron: The Master Serapis Bey

Colour: Selenite White

Shape: The Two Pillars

Properties: Flow, the path of least resistance, acceptance, and intuition. Go with the flow! The angelic frequency, communion with Angels, Angelic mediumship, the wisdom of the Angels. Synchronicity, serendipity, Divine guidance, and opportunity. The Divine Gift.

Active Principle: The Flame of Grace

Crystal: Selenite

Affirmation: I AM GRACE

The Master Serapis Bey speaks:

*Divine beings, welcome. You must understand that both your
Guardian Angel and the Angels of the angelic realm are here to
support you.*

*Calling on them and invoking their presence will assist you in
your efforts in this life, this incarnation.*

Remember, they may not interfere with your free will.

*Do ask, do invoke, do request, do pray if you wish and, in this
way, connect to your team in spirit, your Angels, and indeed to my
energy.*

Ask and it is so.

The 3rd Ray
The Ray of New Beginnings

Patron: The Lady Master Nada (Mary Magdalene)

Colour: Rose Pink

Shape: Triangle

Properties: Growth, birth, purity, innocence, and awe. The Inner Child. The wisdom of the Divine Feminine – the Sophia – the Feminine Christ force. The power of sacred sound – the song of creation, love, beauty, empathy, and appreciation.

Active Principle: The Magdalene Flame

Crystal: Rose Quartz

Affirmation: I AM CREATION

The Ascended Master Lady Nada speaks:

Beloved brothers and sisters, this Ray, this energy is both gentle and powerful. It is the Ray of Divine love.

The healing energy of this Ray is akin to water that falls lightly like rain but also in huge waves and torrents as a tsunami.

The feminine energy that this Ray represents is being rebalanced at this time. Balance will return.

Call on us, I, and my brothers and sisters who serve on this Ray will bring you much healing and guidance. I leave you now with love.

The 4th Ray
The Ray of the Spiritual Warrior

Patron: The Master El Morya (King Arthur)

Colour: Royal Blue

Shape: Square

Properties: Stability, physical grounding, strength, strategy, leadership, discipline. Masculine – solar – dynamic force. The way of self-mastery - the way of the spiritual warrior – champion of the light, defender of the weak, the clearing of negative energies and entities. The Will of the Divine.

Active Principle: The Flame of Mastery

Crystal: Sapphire

Affirmation: I AM MASTERY

The Ascended Master El-Morya speaks:

Your will is your God-given right.

Free will is your gift, do not allow others to deprive you of this gift. This will, this free will, supports your life's purpose to live to your potential in this lifetime.

It is the will of the Divine that you experience your life on this planet in this way.

Call me should you need support; call me should you need a warrior to stand by your side. The energy of this Ray will provide you with that which you need.

Live to the best of your ability, waste not this opportunity, dear one.

The 5th Ray
The Ray of Unity

Properties: The Master Kuthumi

(St Francis of Assisi)

Colour: Butter Yellow

Shape: The Pentacle/Pentagon

Properties: Equilibrium and balance, the classical elements, the holistic perspective. Unity consciousness and interconnection, the tapestry of life. Relationships and mediation, the life streams of the world, self-awareness, self-knowledge, internal dialogue. The acknowledgement that the Divine is to be found in all living things.

Active Principle: The Flame of Unification

Crystal: Yellow Kunzite (Spodumene)

Affirmation: I AM UNITY

The Master Kuthumi speaks:

Friends, you are part of all that there is.

Every one of you divine beings is connected, all brothers and sisters, made from the same material, cut from the same cloth as each other.

You would do well to remember this; remember you are a part of the tapestry of life.

Connect with me to remember your place in this world, to remember your connectedness to all that there is, and to remember your true self.

The 6th Ray
The Ray of the Divine Mother

Patron:　　　The Lady Master – Mother Mary

Colour:　　　Madonna Blue

Shape:　　　Hexagram/Hexagon　(Six-Pointed Star)

Properties: Nurturing, healing, unconditional love, evocation, and comfort. The Goddess mysteries, the Divine Mother (Shekinah) and the Tree of Knowledge. Service, duty, purpose, and restraint; self-possession. Introspection, meditation, silence, and retreat – the power of going within. Restoration, rest, and peace.

Active Principle: The Flame of Nurture

Crystal:　　　Sodalite

Affirmation:　　I AM NURTURE

The Lady Master Mary speaks:

Divine children, brothers and sisters, sons, and daughters of light, call on me when you wish to understand your purpose.

Call on me when you wish to feel comfort and security, to feel peace.

Perfect peace is possible within the vibration of this Ray.

Go within, dearest ones, go within.

Listen to what your heart speaks, go within. Listen to what your soul speaks, go within. Listen to the divine speak.

In love and light, I leave you.

The 7th Ray
The Ray of Spiritual Alchemy

Patron: The Master St Germain

Colour: Violet (Amethyst Purple)

Shape: The Heptagon/Heptagram (Seven-Pointed Star)

Properties: Change, transformation, alchemy – clearing and transmutation (the process and journey of change) and its catalytic quickening. Magick, ceremony, ritual, and initiation – perception, vision, clairvoyance and mysticism. Those who 'trigger' others into self-exploration and the possibility of personal change.

Active Principle: The Violet Flame

Crystal: Amethyst

Affirmation: I AM DIVINE ALCHEMY

The Ascended Master St Germain speaks:

Beloveds! The Violet Flame, this Ray of magic, transmutation and alchemy, can enable you to bring about great and sweeping changes in your life.

Used on a regular basis, it will clear psychic debris, support your personal path of development, and enable you to live your best life.

There is much that can be achieved by working with this energy. I would encourage you to invoke this Ray and its energy if, in simple terms, you wish your life to flow with ease and grace; it will be so!

The 8ᵗʰ Ray
The Ray of Harmony

Patron: The Masters Kwan Yin
            & Djwhal Khul

Colour: Jade Green

Shape: Octagon/Octagram (Eight-Pointed Star)

Properties: Chaos leading to order, order leading to chaos –
the swing of the pendulum, the power of opposites, the cycle of
duality and polarity – the lessons of impermanence. The potential
for peace, tranquillity, balance and calm, the constancy of
movement, and eternity. Exorcism, banishment and compassion.

Active Principle: The Flame of Compassion

Crystal: Jade

Affirmation: I AM COMPASSION

The Lady Master Kwan Yin speaks:

Children, there is a place for compassion in order; there is a place for love. Call on me when you wish to elevate the vibration of a discourse, of a relationship, and inject it with the essence of peace and compassion.

You may think that my energy is soft and light, it is, and it is not. It can be as soft as a butterfly's wing or as strong as a Dragon's fire, depending on the requirement.

Call on the Flame of Compassion, invoke the Ray and my presence and that of my brother. It is much needed on the planet at this time.

You may choose to use this energy for yourself or share it with those who need it. In peace, I depart.

The 9th Ray
The Ray of Challenge

Patron: The Lady Master Portia

Colour: Magenta

Shape: Nonagon/Nonagram (Nine-Pointed Star)

Properties: Challenge, initiation, and opportunity. The deep feminine mysteries – magic, mediumship and seership. Transition and passage from one state/place to another – altered states, consciousness/trance. The shadow and its refinement and acceptance (NOT transformation), introspection, psychism, intuition and sensuality (they are connected).

Active Principle: The Silver Violet Flame

Crystal: Sugilite

Affirmation: I AM EMBODIMENT

The Ascended Master Lady Portia speaks:

Beloveds, brothers and sisters of light, understand that the Silver Violet flame has a separate and distinct energy to that of the Violet Flame itself.

It carries deep codes of magic, and these threads of ancient magic reborn in Avalon rise again, held in the hearts of beacons of light on the planet at this time.

Call on me when you wish to bathe in this ethereal light; sit with Sugilite which embodies this energy. Step into the light of this Ray when you experience challenge, call on the Silver Violet flame for support.

Deep dark mysteries await when you explore this Ray. I leave you with my blessings.

The 10th Ray
The Ray of the Divine Father

Patron: Cosmic Ascended Master

Maitreya/the Christ

Colour: Pure White

Symbol: The Sun

Properties: God. The Great Central Sun. The Divine Father, the unified Christ energy (male and female combined as one). Genesis, beginning, the creator energies and codes, union with the source, communion, and emergence. The manifest universe – the created reality of time and space.

Active Principle: The Flame of Divine Order

Crystal: Herkimer Diamond

Affirmation: I AM DIVINE ORDER

The Cosmic Ascended Master Maitreya / The Christ speaks:

Divine souls, each of you is made manifest in the image of the Divine.

Each of you, unique sparks of divinity.

Connect with this Ray when you want to experience communion with the Creator of All.

A merging of your energy with the Divine.

A simple yet powerful opportunity to remember who you truly are.

The 11th Ray
The Green Ray

Patron: The Archangel Uriel

Colour: Green

Symbol: The Trilithon

(An Archway of Three Stones – A Henge)

Properties: The power of the life cycle, birth, life, death, and decay. The harmony of nature, regeneration, restoration, and renaissance. The Earth element and Earth elementals, the healing (and magical) power of herbs, flowers, weeds, plants, and trees. Earth wisdom and magic, abundance, physical health and well-being.

Active Principle: The Green Flame

Crystal: Verdite

Affirmation: I AM AT ONE WITH GAIA

The Archangel Uriel speaks:

Children of Gaia, the energy of this Ray is about growth and healing, healing of the planet, healing from the plant kingdom.

Invoke this Ray to better understand the healing energy of all plants. Invoke this Ray to select those most fitting with your vibration.

Sit within this Ray when you wish to send healing to the plant kingdom, to the planet herself. Call upon my presence for support with this healing; it will be so.

The 20th Ray
The Ray of Miracle

Patron: Cosmic Ascended
                     Master Maha Cohan

Colour: Turquoise Blue

Symbol: The Dove

Properties: Connection, communion, communication, and alignment. Synchronicity, serendipity and attunement, the power of miracle. Divine will, service and the spiritual path, inspiration and the inspirer, spiritual teaching, and spiritual healing. Service and sacrifice and the courage required to do both. The Holy Spirit.

Active Principle: The Flame of Miracle

Crystal: Blue Topaz

Affirmation: I AM MIRACLE

The Cosmic Ascended Master Maha Cohan
speaks:

Beloved, call on the energy of this Ray when you wish to bring a 'sea change', complete change of the situation you are in.

If you invoke this change for the highest good of all, it will be so, it may take some time for the universe to align with your wishes, but be safe in the knowledge that miracles occur.

It is important to be careful not to influence free will as one does not wish to fall foul of the laws of Karma. However, do not allow this fact to prevent you from asking or invoking a change for the highest good of all.

A miracle is simply a manifestation of the highest order for the highest good.

Beloved, do not be afraid or shy of invoking this energy. I leave you with my blessings that you might connect and commune.

The 22nd Ray
The Ray of Healing

Patron: The Archangel Raphael

Colour: Sky Blue

Symbol: The Caduceus

Properties: Communication, expression, creativity, the herald, the messenger. Writing, art, drama, communication technology. Healing, sacred sound, song, mantra, chant. Travel and protection when travelling, navigation and discovery. The air element and elementals, telepathy, and mediumship.

Active Principle: The Flame of Healing

Crystal: Blue Chalcedony

Affirmation: I AM HEALING

The Archangel Raphael speaks:

Beloveds, to some of you I am an old friend. Others not acquainted with my energy, I bid you welcome. You will come to know and regard me as friend and ally.

Call upon me, call upon the energy of this Ray when you wish to channel energy to others. Always, I implore you to ask for the highest and best outcome, to ask for the highest vibration that is possible to aid your friends, your family, your people.

This Ray will assist those who wish to offload their woes, their worries, their cares; to communicate them rather than conceal them. Be not surprised if you use this Ray and channel it for the good of healing that you will be obliged to listen, simply listen as this energy does its work.

There are many purposes for which you can invoke this energy, be aware, dearest one that it also provides protection. I invite you to open your heart and be the channel, be the conduit, be the change that is required.

Ask for my support and I will stand by you and enable this in deepest love.

The 30th Ray
The Ray of Earth Consciousness

Patron: Cosmic Ascended Master Sanat Kumara

Colour: Deep Red

Symbol: Earth Square (Tatwas)

Properties: The bridge to the consciousness of the Earth Spirit Gaia, the High Priest of the Earth Spirit, her ambassador, and translator. All Devas and Elementals (Gnomes, Mountain Devas, Dryads, and plant Devas etc.) the Mineral, Vegetable Kingdom and Animal Kingdoms. Earth Healing, the energy system of the Earth.

Active Principle: The Flame of Life

Crystal: Red Jasper

Affirmation: I AM LIFE

The Cosmic Ascended Master Sanat Kumara speaks:

Child, this energy, this Ray is around you completely, continuously.

Tapping into its energy would be for the reason of increasing its power to support the energy that is already coming forth.

It may be directed, those who already work within this Ray understand this, they understand that they are to be guided by higher powers as to the enhancement they provide.

Should a seeker wish to participate they need to obligate themselves to the guides and guardians of your world, to set aside ego and simply become a channel in service for love of all.

The 33rd Ray
The Ray of Protection

Patron: The Archangel Michael

Colour: Electric Blue

Symbol: The Sword

Properties: Protection, perception and passion, transformation, alchemy, and courage. The warrior of light, spiritual rescue (psychopomp work), entity release, spiritual clearing. The spiritual warrior, motivation, justice, harmony, and Karma. Sensuality, sexuality and attraction, justice, right action, and harmony.

Active Principle: The Flame of Justice

Crystal: Aqua Aura

Affirmation: I AM JUSTICE

The Archangel Michael speaks:

Children of light, call upon me for protection, work with me, support those who need protecting, invoke my energy, let us remove negativity from your world together.

Many call upon me and I respond, you may know that you can benefit from my strength as well as my protection.

You may call upon me to gain strength, to be a better person, to support others as well as your own being.

Children of light, call and I will be with you.

The 40th Ray
The Ray of Law

Patron: Cosmic Ascended Master Moses

Colour: Blue Grey

Symbol: The Crook (The Herald's staff)

Properties: Universal Law, order, harmony, truth, faith, belief. Divine order, the Divine plan, esoteric mechanics, the Spiritual Laws. Guidance – leading by example – the living of the spiritual life, the spiritual path. Hope, inspiration, miracle and magic, salvation, escape, the leader and advocate.

Active Principle: The Flame of Accord

Crystal: Lithium Quartz

Affirmation: I AM ACCORD

The Cosmic Ascended Master Moses speaks:

Beloved children, you are invited to connect with me and the energy of this Ray; this energy stands for right, for justice, for accord.

Call upon this Ray in order to build relationships and maintain them. Understand there is order required, see as a man leads a flock of sheep, he catches the errant one with his crook, returning it to the flock. As mankind has become separate and separated, accord has become more difficult.

This balance can be returned by invoking my support for your leaders, so that they lead by example rather than as puppets and bowing to other masters who do not have the best intention for the peoples, who have their own agenda.

Call my support, call the energy of this Ray for diplomats, for politicians, for all of those in power that they may be guided appropriately that they may be guided to fulfil the best for their peoples.

Should you, dearest one, wish to lead, call me for support, call me for guidance, call me to support your wisdom, call me to lead with dignity and integrity and in the highest good of all.

The 44th Ray
The Ray of Birth

Patron: The Archangel Gabriel

Colour: Aquamarine

Symbol: The Chalice

Properties: Dreams, the Moon, messages and messengers, flow, grace, cleansing and synchronicity. Intuition, visions, clairvoyance and psychism. The astral planes and astral travel, magical manifestation. Sacred sound and resurrection. The water element and elementals, the unconscious mind, and its powers!

Active Principle: The Flame of Life

Crystal: Aquamarine

Affirmation: I AM FLOW

The Archangel Gabriel speaks:

Beloved, I am the Angel of Water, and it is fitting that Aquamarine is used to connect with my energy. I can support you with raising your vibration, with accessing those erstwhile hidden dreams, intuitive connections, and connections with all on the astral planes.

Seek my support when you wish to tap into those unused aspects of yourself. Invoke my support to benefit others as well as yourself, for always with the highest intention you can make this request.

Dearest one, the message I bring you is that you are loved, remember that.

The 50th Ray
The Ray of Wisdom

Patron: The Cosmic Ascended Master Solomon

Colour: Gold

Symbol: A Golden Ring (to wear upon the finger)

Properties: Wisdom, wisdom in action, spiritual leadership, rulership, and command. Esoteric and spiritual knowledge and truth, the intellect in combination with intuition, comprehension, spiritual and magical laws, and spiritual mechanics. Angelic communion and magic, the Merkabah and dimensional travel.

Active Principle: The Flame of Wisdom

Crystal: Golden Calcite

Affirmation: I AM WISDOM

The Cosmic Ascended Master Solomon speaks:

This flame, this Flame of Wisdom, is permanently shining brightly; those who are seekers may tap into its guidance, those who pray are guided here, those who ask and invoke, find this wisdom accessible to them.

It is not for the faint of heart when you invoke this energy. Its wisdom will fill your consciousness to the exclusion of all else. It will allow you to tap into those spiritual and esoteric truths for which mankind seeks support which are and always have been available.

Support is always here. You may prefer, if you so wish, to ask your guides and guardians to seek this information for you rather than bringing it about yourself; it may feel more comfortable for your energy body to do so. Those of you of sufficient vibration may seek guidance, may be enlightened with truth.

All of this knowledge is available for all of mankind, the seeker must seek with an open heart with good intention, only then will this wisdom become available.

Blessed ones, seek and ye shall find.

The 55th Ray
The Ray of Endings and Beginnings

Patron: The Archangel Azrael

Colour: Black

Symbol: The Scythe

Properties: Death and rebirth, incarnation, the Akashic Records, past lives, Karma, karmic cleansing, tie cutting and healing. Remembrance and restoration, the quintessential spiritual force of life, the Void. Time and cycles, inner light, creation – the progenitor, mystery, and magic. The Akashic element and elementals.

Active Principle: The Flame of the Akasha

Crystal: Hypersthene

Affirmation: I AM THE CIRCLE OF LIFE

The Archangel Azrael speaks:

Children of Light, all that is and has been, is recorded for your benefit, for the benefit of all.

It is accessible to all*, request an audience with one of the guides by tuning into this Ray, asking me to draw by your side, and seeing me cut through all irrelevant information.

In this way you can go directly to the information and the guidance that is required by you or the person you seek it for. This Ray will fall about you with ease if the information you seek is for the purpose of good.

Be advised, do not use this information to affect the will of another; this will rebound on you, the Karma will take many lives to dissolve.

Be true, be of right thinking, when you enter these halls. I will guide, I will support, invoke my presence, seek and you shall find.

*refers to the Halls of the Akasha

The 60th Ray
The Ray of the Priestess

Patron: Cosmic Lady Ascended Master Isis

Colour: Malachite Green

Symbol: The Crescent Moon

Properties: The Divine Feminine, wisdom power and magic; the magic and wisdom of the Moon. Motherhood, nurture, protection and healing, the mother's love. The power of the wife, the healer, resurrection, foresight, prophecy, oracle, silence, and stillness.

Active Principle: The Flame of Receptivity

Crystal: Lapis Lazuli

Affirmation: I AM STILL

The Cosmic Lady Ascended Master Isis speaks:

Sisters and brothers, understand that when working within the energy of this Ray much is possible.

First, find a contemplative space within yourself and then invoke my presence, in doing so many of you will remember your times spent in my presence and in the temples dedicated to me; remember the healing power of these temples, the sacred oils and sound used.

Sisters and brothers, the energy of the divine feminine can be dark and mysterious. I bring the energy of the moon. Sit with me, sisters and brothers, if you wish your Soul to experience deep and nurturing space.

I will welcome you, hold you in the stillness, I will sit with you, dearest sisters and brothers, and hold your hand while you experience the energy of this Ray and all its possibilities.

The 66th Ray
The Ray of Unconditional Love

Patron: The Archangel Haniel

Colour: Kunzite Pink

Symbol: The Heart

Properties: Unconditional love, the awakening of the Higher Heart, compassion, mercy, love and empathy. The way and wisdom of the Divine Mother, forgiveness, absolution, repentance (as in turning towards the Divine). Connection to the tapestry of life, animal communication, emotional healing.

Active Principle: The Flame of Cosmic Love

Crystal: Kunzite

Affirmation: ALL IS LOVE

The Archangel Haniel speaks:

Beloveds, I would encourage you to sit within the energy of this Ray to experience the love of the Divine. This Ray, this love, flows throughout this Galaxy, this Universe. There are many different forms of love vibration, the love of the Creator is the highest.

Beloveds, step into this Ray and bathe in the love of the Creator; bathe in the purest unconditional love.

Sit within this field of energy, this Ray, to experience bliss. All can use and invoke this energy for the self and others; share it, channel it and bathe others in its purity.

It is simple and accessible to all, invoke my presence, open your heart to feel the love of the creator.

The 70th Ray
The Ray of Magic

Patron: The Cosmic Ascended Master Merlin

Colour: The Dark Rainbow (Labradorite)

Symbol: The Wand

Properties: Magic, arcane wisdom, magical law and truth – magical correspondence. Service, knowledge, intelligence, and comprehension. The impossible and improbable – the cosmic trickster, initiator, and challenger – rites of passage. Sight and vision, prophecy, and divination – fortune and destiny!

Active Principle: The Flame of True Magic

Crystal: Labradorite

Affirmation: I AM ORIGINAL MAGIC

The Cosmic Ascended Master Merlin speaks:

Brothers and sisters, this is the Ray of the seer, this is the Ray of divination, of prophecy. The Ray of true magic, true raw and unbridled magic. Call upon this Ray with great care, use this magical Ray with discernment and wisdom; with knowledge that this true magic can influence all.

Be advised, knowledge of the spiritual laws would be preferable before undertaking any true magic. Consult my brother, the Ascended Master Solomon, if you are in any doubt. The Karmic ramifications may be great otherwise.

Those of you true in heart who wish to bring magic to your world for the betterment of mankind are welcome to call upon my energy, the energy of this Ray.

Sit within this Ray to feel the power of true magic to feel its energy move within your blood, your physical and subtle bodies.

What fun we can have together, but there is a very serious side to true magic - handle with care, brothers and sisters!

The 77th Ray
The Ray of Evolution

Patron: The Archangel Samael

Colour: Blood Red

Symbol: The World Tree (The Tree of Life)

Properties: Change, evolution, ascension, movement, impermanence, growth, cycle, expansion, unfoldment. The 12-strand DNA, the Tree of Life, the Celtic World Tree – the Anima Mundi – spine of the world. Motivation, passion, criticism, perspective, and opinion. Challenger and those who trigger others. The shadow self, sacrifice.

Active Principle: The Flame of Ascension

Crystal: Garnet

Affirmation: I AM EVOLUTION

The Archangel Samael speaks:

Children, beloveds, you are all connected to all that there is, everything within this Universe is such. The make-up of your physical self is recycled. All is recycled, reused, reborn as your planet has evolved. This is a part of the cycle of evolution.

Call upon the energies of this Ray when you seek to find the reason for change, when you work behind the human I, with your shadow self. Invoke my presence, this Ray, for support with such endeavours.

Sit beneath the World Tree for support, amongst this energy for a deeper understanding of evolution and change. To understand what has gone before and what is to come.

The 80th Ray
The Ray of Order

Patron: The Cosmic Ascended Master Lord Kahn

Colour: Diamond White

Symbol: The Blossoming Lotus

Properties: Harmony, peace, order, resolution, equilibrium, balance, calm. Stillness – the zero point. Restoration, realignment to the Divine and the spiritual path, the way shower and herald – those who lead by example. Mediator and counsellor. The Ray of peacekeepers, healing, sanctuary, home and retreat.

Active Principle: The Flame of Order

Crystal: Girasol Quartz

Affirmation: I AM HARMONY

The Cosmic Ascended Master Lord Kahn speaks:

Seekers, these are very simple words*, very apt and true words, for only when you know thyself can you seek to help and support others.

I am Lord Kahn. Connect with this Ray when you wish to find stillness and peace, the light of the Divine. The light of the Divine welcomes seekers of light.

This Ray, this energy, affects a contemplative state beloved. You are all capable of reaching such a state. Discipline, dedication, and trust are required of the disciple who awaits guidance from the Divine. The energy of this Ray will also enable seekers to better connect with the Angelic Realm.

*refers to the affirmation

The 88th Ray
The Ray of Commonality
(Divine Love)

Patron: The Archangelic Collective The Cherubim

Colour: Deep Pink

Symbol: The Flaming Heart

Properties: The tapestry of love, the connecting thread that binds all things together through the love of their creator. The first web of all, the fabric of the Universe, affinity through love, empathy, compassion, community, and commonality of feeling. Sympathy, charity and mercy, forgiveness and second chances.

Active Principle: The Flame of Divine Love in All

Crystal: Pink Sapphire

Affirmation: I AM DIVINE LOVE

The Archangelic Collective The Cherubim speak:

Sweet children, the Universe is created of love, All is created of love, you are part of that love, you are connected to that love. Sit within the energy of this Ray when you feel you wish to experience that love.

Sit within the energy of this Ray when you wish to feel part of All that there is. Sit within the energy of this Ray, bring it down in waves around you when you wish support with forgiveness and compassion for your fellow man. Sit within the energy of this Ray for the greater good of all.

Bring this Ray about you when you wish to connect with your fellow man for the greater good of all. Send your intention through these invisible threads of light to those that need healing, whose vibration needs to be lifted in universal love.

You are love, crafted with love by the Creator, be that love.

BE ONLY LOVE.

The 90th Ray
The Ray of the Cosmic Divine Mother

Patron: The Cosmic Lady Ascended Master Annami

Colour: Deep Blue Black

Symbol: The Black Rose

Properties: The Void, the beginning of all, chaotic ocean of infinite potential, the impossible chaos. Priestess of the Great Cosmic Mother. Dreaming and communion through dreams. Original magic and creation, healing the Soul, transcendence of Universal Law and limitation. Silence and absence and stillness.

Active Principle: The Black Flame of the Void

Crystal: Jet

Affirmation: I AM INFINITE

The Cosmic Lady Ascended Master
Annami speaks:

Sisters and brothers, when you connect with this Ray you will understand your dreams better.

The Void is the primordial lake of creation. Travel to this space and bathe in it when you wish your Soul to be healed.

Cleanse yourself in its energy, experience stillness.

The 99th Ray
The Ray of Interconnection

Patron: The Archangelic Collective The Seraphim

Colour: Pale Champagne Gold

Symbol: The Flower of Life

Properties: The tapestry of life, the connecting thread that binds all things together through commonality of origin – the Divine. The second web of all, the fabric of the Universe, interconnection, alignment, the spiritual path and synchronicity. Communion and higher vibrational mediumship, shamanic unity consciousness.

Active Principle: The Flame of Universal Consciousness

Crystal: Seraphinite

Affirmation: I AM CONNECTED TO ALL

The Archangelic Collective the Seraphim speak:

Sisters and brothers, brothers and sisters, you are one. The energy of this Ray supports your connection to the Angelic Realm, your connection to all of the Realms of Light.

Call upon this Ray when you wish to commune, call upon this Ray for guidance, for information, all will be really revealed to those of you pure in heart; the seeker who seeks the information for the highest good of all will be welcomed.

We are connected, you are connected, all are connected, lean back into this connection, feel it holding you in your space and place at this time. See and feel the energy of the Divine moving about this web of interconnectedness and feel its comfort, feel its love, feel its strength.

Brothers and sisters, sisters and brothers, we are one, you are one, aspects, fragments, splinters, of Divine Consciousness.

Remember this.

The 100th Ray
The Ray of Time

Patron: The Archangelic Collective The Elohim

Colour: Lepidolite Blue (Glittering Pale Blue)

Symbol: The Infinity Loop (Lemniscate)

Properties: Time, infinity, cosmic time, timelessness, time travel. The qualities of time, love, grace, mercy – precognition and retrocognition – time suspension, bloating time, shrinking time. History remembered and lost, the mystery of the beginning (and ending) of all. The constraint of miracle and the working of miracle.

Active Principle: The Flame of Cosmic Time

Crystal: Lepidolite

Affirmation: I AM INFINITY

The Archangelic Collective the Elohim speak:

Beloveds, time is a human construct. Should you invoke the energy of this Ray it will become apparent that all is not as it seems. With the best intentions you can influence time, stop time, expand time - with the highest intention, this is possible. All beings are subject to the spiritual laws; however, with the highest intention, you can stretch and influence time.

We have served from the beginning and continue to do so. Understand if your intention is a life of service, then you will be gifted the ability to influence time. Those whose souls are born under this Ray will understand this.

Sit within the energy of this Ray, call upon it to experience moving through time, both forward and backward, the energy of this Ray will support you, beloveds.

Part Four

Soul Lessons

"The students should at all times remember that no matter what their mistakes may have been, God never criticizes nor condemns them; but at every stumble which is made, in that sweet, loving Voice says:

"Arise, My Child, and try again, and keep on trying, until at last you have attained the True Victory and Freedom of your God-given Dominion."

St. Germain, The "I AM" Discourses
Guy Ballard 1935

A Final Message from
the Patrons of the Divine Rays

"Beloveds, you have at your fingertips information that can support both your spiritual development and ascension, gifts that can support the wellbeing and healing of all that there is.

We ask that you use these gifts with the best and highest intention for good. Be aware that the spiritual laws, the laws of Karma, of cause and effect, will be brought into play should you misuse these gifts.

We, the Ascended Master Collective, we the patrons of these Divine Rays, will draw close and support you when your intention is for the highest good.

In love, we leave you beloved, holding the light of the Divine Rays."

The Ascended Master El Morya
Channelled by Angela Orora, April 2021

Awakening

I'd like to share a little more about my personal spiritual journey with you.

My faith in the Creator and inner knowledge that we are all connected has been part of me for as long as I can remember and after moving from Wales, I spent a decade exploring different aspects, different spiritual pathways and learning to trust my own intuition.

For most of us, as children, we are tuned in intuitively, but sadly our societal 'programming' and the ego step in and cloud our inner knowing with doubt.

I have made some terrible decisions based on logic and taken some wonderful, seemingly 'crazy' leaps of faith based on intuition. None of this is wrong; this life we are experiencing is all about choice. Every decision we make, every relationship we have brings learning and sometimes hard lessons. All of those make you who you are, a unique soul on their own path of learning and development.

On balance, hand on heart, I would say that the intuitive decisions have served me best. One of these intuitive decisions led me to agree to being the channel for this book. As I've said before, I don't consider myself to be special in any way; I simply decided that I wished to serve humanity.

I have thousands of spiritual experiences that I could share with you, and perhaps I'll write about them one day, but there is one lesson I learned many years ago that I feel is very important to share with you now.

It was winter, London, 1985, and I had signed up for a Tarot Reading course. My teacher was absolutely lovely but was wholly inexperienced and really didn't know what to do with me! Basically, as soon as I started meditating, energy was flowing through me so fast that when I placed my hands in water, it bubbled as if boiling. My clairvoyance turned on like the flick of a switch, and I became super-sensitive to energy, so much so that I was experiencing the physical pain from people several feet away from me on the Tube and picking up emotions of those in turmoil around me.

I had opened up spiritually, or 'awakened' as we say today, but had not been taught how to shield myself, protect my energetic system from external influences.

After about two weeks, my lovely teacher referred me to her own teacher, the wonderful Betty Balcombe, whom I mentioned earlier. I spent seven years 'in circle' with Betty (she went on to write several books on psychic development), and I consider myself truly blessed to be one of her students.

Over thirty-five years later, the world is a very different place. We all have access to information at our fingertips that can assist spiritual awakening. What concerns me is that a lot of this information is incomplete, not all are backed up by experience, and there is a host of 'spiritual teachers' and coaches who, like my lovely inexperienced first teacher, will offer to guide you with the best will in the world.

Please, please, dearest soul, remember to invoke protection before beginning any spiritual practice. This was a lesson I learned the hard way!

I wish you every blessing on your journey of discovery, of remembrance and spiritual growth. You are a divine being; I hope that this journey will help you to remember the divine Soul you truly are.

A Bit About Crystals

Crystals, crystal care, and crystal healing are yet another huge subject that I will not even attempt to discuss in detail; I have referenced excellent authors earlier in the book and their details can be found in the Bibliography.

Very simply, as I said at the very beginning, scientists agree that everything in this Universe has a unique vibration. It then follows that every rock, stone, or crystalline form has a unique vibration. This vibration is unique for three reasons, the molecular structure, the spirit or deva that inhabits the crystal, and the interdimensional power source of crystals.

The best description I have found to help you understand these concepts is in *Crystals to Go* by Edwin Courtenay; there is also a chapter on etheric crystals in this book, and you can save yourself an enormous amount of money, and the planet and crystal kingdom much less disturbance, by accessing crystal energy in this way.

Crystals are fantastic allies in any spiritual work. When you begin working with the Divine Rays, allying and aligning yourself to crystal energy can be of tremendous benefit. Please make sure that any crystals you use are ethically sourced and that you cleanse, attune, and charge them appropriately in order that they may support you energetically.

I believe that crystals choose you rather than the other way around, and so I have put the information about the Divine Rays into a handy table format so that if your crystal calls out to you on a particular day, you can easily find the Ray that its energy is aligned to.

Quick Reference: The Divine Rays Alphabetically by Crystal

Crystal	Ray	Shape/Symbol	Colour	Patron	The Ray of	Active Principle
Amethyst	7	The Heptagon/ Heptagram (7-Pointed Star)	Violet	The Master St Germain	Spiritual Alchemy	The Violet Flame
Aqua Aura	33	The Sword	Electric Blue	The Archangel Michael	Protection	The Flame of Justice
Aquamarine	44	The Chalice	Aquamarine	The Archangel Gabriel	Birth	The Flame of Life
Blue Chalcedony	22	The Caduceus	Sky Blue	The Archangel Raphael	Healing	The Flame of Healing
Blue Topaz	20	The Dove	Turquoise Blue	Cosmic Ascended Master Maha Cohan	Miracle	The Flame of Miracle
Garnet	77	The World Tree (Tree of Life)	Blood Red	The Archangel Samael	Ascension	The Flame of Evolution
Girasol Quartz	80	The Blossoming Lotus	Diamond White	Cosmic Ascended Master Lord	Order	The Flame of Order
Golden Calcite	50	A Gold Ring (To Wear Upon One's Finger)	Gold	Cosmic Ascended Master Solomon	Wisdom	The Flame of Wisdom
Herkimer Diamond	10	The Sun	Pure White	Cosmic Ascended Master Maitreya/the Christ	The Divine Father	The Flame of Divine Order

Crystal	Ray	Shape/Symbol	Colour	Patron	The Ray of	Active Principle
Hypersthene	55	The Scythe	Black	The Archangel Azrael	Endings and Beginnings	The Flame of the Akasha
Jade	8	Octagon/Octagram (8-Pointed Star)	Jade Green	The Masters Kwan Yin and Dwal Khul	Harmony	The Flame of Compassion
Jet	90	The Black Rose	Deep Blue Black	Cosmic Lady Ascended Master Annami	The Cosmic Divine Mother	The Black Flame of the Void
Kunzite	66	The Heart	Kunzite Pink	The Archangel Haniel	Unconditional Love	The Flame of Cosmic Love
Labradorite	70	The Wand	The Dark Rainbow (Labradorite)	The Cosmic Ascended Master Merlin	Magic	The Flame of True Magic
Lapis Lazuli	60	The Crescent Moon	Malachite Green	Cosmic Lady Ascended Master Isis	The Ray of the Priestess	The Flame of Receptivity
Lepidolite	100	The Infinity Loop (Lemniscate)	Lepidolite Blue (Glittering Pale Blue)	The Archangelic Collective	Cosmic Time	The Flame of Cosmic Time
Lithium Quartz	40	The Crook (The Herald's Staff)	Blue Grey	Cosmic Ascended Master Moses	Accord	The Flame of Accord

Crystal	Ray	Shape/Symbol	Colour	Patron	The Ray of	Active Principle
Pink Sapphire	88	The Flaming Heart	Deep Pink	The Archangelic Collective The Cherubim	Commonality (Divine Love)	The Flame of Divine Love in All
Red Jasper	30	Earth Square (Tatwas)	Deep Red	Cosmic Ascended Master Sanat Kumara	Earth Consciousness	The Flame of Life
Rose Quartz	3	Triangle	Rose Pink	The Lady Master Nada (Mary Magdalene)	New Beginnings	The Magdalene Flame
Ruby	1	Single Pillar	Red	Master Jesus/Sananda	The Avatar	The Flame of Divine Service
Sapphire	4	Square	Royal Blue	The Master El Morya (King Arthur)	The Spiritual Warrior	The Flame of Mastery
Selenite	2	The Two Pillars	Selenite White	Master Serapis Bey	Grace	The Flame of Grace
Seraphinite	99	The Flower of Life	Champagne Gold	The Archangelic Collective The Seraphim	Interconnection	The Flame of Universal Consciousness
Sodalite	6	Hexagon	Madonna Blue	Lady Master Mother Mary	The Divine Mother	The Flame of Nature
Sugilite	9	Nonagon/Nonagram (9-Pointed Star	Magenta	The Lady Master Portia	Challenge	The Silver Violet Flame
Crystal	Ray	Shape/Symbol	Colour	Patron	The Ray of	Active Principle
Verdite	11	The Trilithon (3 Stones Creating an Archway – a Henge)	Green	The Archangel Uriel	The Green Ray	The Green Flame
Yellow Kunzite	5	Pentagram/Pentacle	Butter Yellow	The Master Khutumi (St Francis of Assisi)	Unity	The Flame of Unification

97

Thank You!

I would like to thank the multitude of spiritual teachers that have inspired me on my path:

Edwin Courtenay, Cunning Man, clairvoyant, channel, and spiritual teacher whose guidance, generosity and grace continue to inspire me. To Edwin, my deepest thanks for his channellings that are referenced within this work.

Betty Balcombe, my dear friend, teacher, and mentor whose love and humour inspired and encouraged me and built the foundation of my spiritual path.

Ted Robinson, whose unfailing encouragement helped me believe in myself.

Mary Banks, the Angel Lady of Merlin's Bridge, my dear friend, and teacher who looked after me while I channelled the majority of this book.

Diana Savil, my dear friend, whose soul shines brightly, channelling the light.

Kieron Morgan, Brother of Dragons, dear friend and colleague who designed the beautiful illustrations of the Divine Ray symbols, your skill and vision is inspiring.

To the wonderful souls and soul sisters that supported my channelling, Nydia Laysa Stone, Angie Evans, Bev Emery, Dr Joan E Howell, Sarah Louise Powell and Rebecca Daniels.

To the amazing spirit-sent team of people whose comments have helped this manuscript shine, Eva Andrea and Debs Byers, Maj, Elin, Linda, Lene, Helen, Anna and Ellen the beta-readers from Eva's Magical Writers Tribe and the fabulous Michelle Emerson, editor and publisher extraordinaire!

Finally, my gratitude to all those souls who throughout this life have helped me learn many lessons.

Thank you Thank You Thank You

Bibliography

Alice Bailey - *A Treatise on the Seven Rays* and other titles

Betty Balcombe – *As I See It* and other titles

Guy Ballard (Godfre Ray King) – *The I AM Discourses* and other titles

Helena Blavatsky – *The Secret Doctrine* and other titles

Edgar Cayce – *The Case for Reincarnation* and other titles

Edwin Courtenay - *Reflections, The Masters Remember, The Archangelic Book of Ritual and Prayer, The Ascended Master Book of Ritual and Prayer, Ascension to Go, Angels to Go, Crystals to Go* and other titles. (http://edwincourtenay.co.uk/books.php)

Shakti Gawain – *Creative Visualisation* and other titles

Judy Hall – *The Crystal Bible (Volumes 1-3)* and other titles

Aurelia Louise Jones - *The Seven Sacred Flames*

Caitlin Matthews - *The Psychic Protection Handbook: Powerful protection for Uncertain Times*

Philip Permutt – *The Crystal Healer* and other titles

Vianna Stabil - *Seven Planes of Existence: The Philosophy of The Theta Healing Technique* and other titles

Glossary

Affirmations

The use of commands or instructions that can be used to change the internal programming of the unconscious mind.

Angel

A spiritual being superior to humans in power and intelligence especially, one in the lowest rank in the celestial hierarchy.

Archeia

A female archangel, the divine feminine aspect of an archangel.

Archangel

A chief or senior angel in the celestial hierarchy, usually regarded as male.

Ascended Master

Member of the Brotherhood, an enlightened being who has completed their incarnations on Earth and resolved their Karma and chosen to help those who remain on Earth.

Ascension

A process of personal and global evolution.

Ascension Symptoms

Physical side effects felt in different ways by different people as a result of ascension waves.

Aspect

A fragment of either an Ascended Master or Archangelic consciousness which is given individual existence and incarnated on Earth.

Celestial Hierarchy

A traditional hierarchy of angels ranked from lowest to highest into the following nine orders: angels, archangels, principalities, powers, virtues, dominions, thrones, cherubim, and seraphim.

Channel

A medium who receives information and communication, either through trance, clairvoyance, clairaudient or clairsentient from the spirit world and spiritual hierarchy.

Channelling

The act of bringing forth either through trance, using 'clair' senses or telepathic connection, messages from the spiritual worlds.

Cosmic Ascended Masters

A higher version of the ascended master collective containing beings who have moved on from the Ascended Masters to watch over more cosmic occurrences.

Cosmic Ascended Master Collective

Includes the three first souls to be created: Sanat Kumara, the Maitreya and the Maha Cohan.

Crystal Deva

Deva means spirit - 'shining one' in Sanskrit.

Etheric Crystal

The etheric imprint of crystal energy without the crystal being physically present.

Invocation

The act or process of petitioning for help or support.

Mala beads

A string of 108 beads traditionally used to count repetitions of mantra.

Mantra

A phrase in English or other language spoken, chanted or sung repetitively to bring changes to the consciousness or reality.

Numerology

The study of the occult significance of numbers.

Occult

Not easily apprehended or understood, hidden from view.

Prayer

An address (such as a petition) to God or a god in word or thought.

Spiritual Protection

A request made to spiritual guides or guardians by way of prayer, ritual, or invocation to protect a space or person before commencing any spiritual work.

Transpersonal Chakras

Chakras that are not part of the physical body (particularly The Stellar Gateway, Soul Star and Earth Star Chakras).

The White Brotherhood or Lodge

Another name for the Ascended Masters.

Other Work by Angela Orora

Angela serves the world under the banner of Cariad Spiritual. Her logo illustrates her belief that we all have the ability to transform and 'Be The Butterfly', soaring and reaching into the flower of life to embrace 'All that there is'.

Life & Soul Alignment Coaching

Angela has supported private clients worldwide for many years. Her unique Life & Soul Alignment Coaching process weaves together traditional life coaching and holistic energy techniques, aligning you to your soul connection and achieving harmony and flow in all areas of mind, body and spirit. Enabling you to soar in all areas of your life and work with grace and flow and a deep connection to source energy.

Ascension Numerology, Channelled Readings, Healing & Spiritual Consultations

Angela offers a range of services to private clients internationally tailored to individual requirements.

Cariad Spiritual Academy offers accredited training in intuitive development, energy healing and spiritual growth, designed to support you to soar, reclaim your sovereign self and 'Be The Butterfly'.

Cariad Spiritual & Halcyon Retreats offer intensive, immersive experiences in beautiful locations worldwide, empowering you with practical tools for spiritual growth in a safe, nurturing space.

Cariad Spiritual Sacred Energy Therapeutics are energetic essential oil blends charged with crystal, sound, and healing energy created to support specific healing issues and spiritual development. A Divine Ray Connection range is also available – see **https://www.cariadspiritual.com/divinerays**.

Find out more at www.cariadspiritual.com

Divine Energy International is a charity supporting the spread of energy healing worldwide, a membership organisation and platform for learning and development in different energy healing modalities.

Angela is a founder member and Chair of the Board of Trustees, our vision is: *A World Where Divine Energy Is For All.*

Find out more at www.divineenergyinternational.org

Other Titles

Angela is also a featured author in two Amazon Best Selling Books Series.

The Wellness Universe Complete Guide to Self-Care: 25 Tools for Goddesses (Published December 2021).

Awaken Your Inner Truth: A Journey of Riches (Published April 2022).

About the Author

Angela Orora Medway-Smith is a Welsh-born spiritual channel and teacher who has been the conduit for healing for thousands of people worldwide.

Her early life was filled with many experiences of death, igniting a deep understanding of the cycle of life.

Angela has had successful careers in both the charity and corporate world alongside her healing work. Her passion for bringing holistic healing to her community led her to create Mind Body Spirit festivals and fayres in Wales, raising thousands of pounds for local children's charities.

Serving under the banner of Cariad Spiritual, Angela is 'The Practical Mystic' a trusted spiritual channel, teacher and Life & Soul Alignment Coach with a long-standing international client base.

Angela first taught intuitive development and healing in Australia in 1990 and now teaches energy healing and spiritual development courses in person, online and at retreat centres worldwide.

Angela lives in South Wales with her husband and family.

Printed in Great Britain
by Amazon

69662488R00068